Old Jack's Ghost Stories from Wales

I Talk You Talk Press

CONTENTS

ACKNOWLEDGMENTS

With sincere thanks to Colin Dixon who collected and recorded the stories contained in this volume. Without his contribution this book would not have been possible.

MESSAGE FROM OLD JACK

I welcome readers old and new to my fifth book of ghost stories. In this book we visit Wales, a country in the United Kingdom.

Wales is a small country, but culturally it is very rich. It has beautiful scenery - wonderful coastlines, deep valleys and high mountains. The people who settled in Wales brought their myths and folk tales with them, and created a land of legends. Of course, Wales' long history hides some dark secrets too. Many of its castles and old pubs and hotels have ghosts. These spirits from the past remind us of the country's long and often tragic history.

Wales has many myths, stories and legends, so it is no surprise that the national flag of Wales has a dragon on it. So come, let the dragon lead you to Wales, where I am ready to tell you some of the country's most mysterious secrets.

1. THE BEAUTY OR THE BEAST?

Place: Carew Castle, Tenby, Pembrokeshire

Our first story is from Pembrokeshire in south west Wales. Pembrokeshire has a wonderful coastline. It is very popular with families, especially in summer. The beaches are beautiful and clean, and it is one of the sunniest parts of Britain. I visited Pembrokeshire in the middle of summer, when the sky and the sea were deep blue, and the beaches were full of tourists. But I didn't visit Pembrokeshire for its bright sunshine and beaches. No, I was more interested in the darker side of Pembrokeshire. I wanted to visit one of Wales' most mysterious and frightening places - Carew Castle.

It was a beautiful hot day, and I decided to walk to the castle. On the way, I became thirsty so I stopped at a small pub.

I went in, ordered a whisky and sat at the bar next to a man about the same age as me. He smiled.

"Beautiful day, isn't it?" he said.

"Yes, it is. Perfect for a walk."

"Where are you going?" he asked.

"To Carew Castle," I said. "I heard the castle has some interesting ghosts."

"Ah!" said the man. "Yes, it does. It's about a thousand years old, so it has many ghosts." He finished his beer and ordered another one.

"So, do you want to see the white lady?" he asked.

"The white lady? Who is she?" I asked.

The man took a long drink of his beer.

"She is the most beautiful woman in Wales," he said. "No, to tell the truth, she is the most beautiful woman in Britain! She's nine hundred years old now, but she hasn't changed. She is still beautiful! Her name is Princess Nest."

"Tell me about her," I said.

"She was the daughter of a king. When she became a woman, she had to marry a man called Gerald de Windsor. She was not happy about it. She had never met Gerald. But she was forced to marry him.

"So the princess and Gerald got married and lived in Carew Castle. The princess grew to love Gerald, and they were happy. They had five children. But one night, everything changed."

"What happened?" I asked.

"Well, one night, Princess Nest was at a banquet. There, she met a man called Owain. He was the son of a Welsh prince. When Owain saw the princess, he fell in love. She was so beautiful. She was the most beautiful woman he had ever seen. He said to himself, 'I want her to be mine. I want to marry her.'"

"But of course, he couldn't. She was already married to Gerald," I said.

"Well, nine hundred years ago, things were different," said the man. "Owain gathered many soldiers and supporters, and one night, they attacked the castle. Of course, Gerald, Princess Nest and the children were very shocked. They couldn't stop Owain and his men. Of course, they wanted to protect the children. Gerald escaped with the children, but the princess didn't have time to escape, and Owain caught her."

"Oh no! She must have been very frightened," I said.

The man smiled, then he said quietly, "Well, some people think she was pleased. Some people say she wanted to go with Owain!"

"Oh," I said. "So it was complicated!"

"Yes, it was. So, Owain took her to Cilgerran Castle, and she lived there with him. They had two children together."

"But what about Gerald?" I asked.

"Well, of course, he wanted to rescue his wife. It took him six years to rescue her. He killed Owain and took Princess Nest back to his castle. He was happy, but a year later, he died."

"What happened to Princess Nest?" I asked.

"She married someone else. But not long after, she died too."

"She had a tragic life," I said.

"Yes, she did. And she still has a tragic life."

"What do you mean?"

"Well, many people have seen her ghost. They say she is a young woman, in a long white dress. People say the woman floats in the air. Maybe she is walking on a high floor of the castle. The castle is old now, so the roof and many of the higher floors are not there anymore. They see a very bright white light around the woman. They say that the woman walks up and down, and she seems very upset."

"Does the ghost stay a long time?" I asked.

"Sometimes around ten minutes. Many people from this village have seen her. They say it is the ghost of Princess Nest. Maybe she is waiting for Gerald, or maybe she is looking for her children."

"Have you seen her?" I asked.

"No, I haven't. But I'd like to. The most beautiful woman in Britain? Of course I'd like to see her!"

I laughed. I looked at my watch.

"It's getting late. I'd better go now. I'm walking to the castle," I said.

I said goodbye to my new friend and walked out of the pub. I walked along the road through the beautiful green fields. In the distance I could see Carew Castle.

It doesn't look scary on a beautiful day like this, I thought.

I bought my ticket at the castle and walked around the castle grounds alone. I looked up and tried to imagine the ghost of Princess Nest. Behind me there was a tour group. The guide was telling the tourists the story of Princess Nest. Then, he said, "But there is a much more frightening story."

Of course, I stood next to the tour group and listened very carefully! This is the story.

In the 17th century, the castle was owned by a man called Sir Rowland Rhys. He was not a nice man. He had a pet monkey. He called the monkey Satan. Rhys often had dinner parties at the castle. He was often very drunk at these parties. He trained his pet monkey to laugh in an evil manner. At the dinner parties, the monkey laughed at the guests. All the guests were very frightened of the monkey.

One very stormy and windy night, a man came to the castle. He lived on the land near the castle. Rhys owned that land. The man had come to pay the rent. Unfortunately, the man didn't have enough money to pay all the rent. Rhys was very angry. He shouted to his monkey Satan, "Attack him! Kill him!"

The monkey laughed and ran towards the man. The man tried to run away, but the monkey was too fast. He was very strong. He attacked the man violently, and nearly killed him. Luckily, some servants in the house helped the man and took him to their room.

Then, the servants and the man heard evil laughter and screaming coming from the dining hall.

"What was that?" asked one of the servants.

"I don't know," said another servant. "Let's go and find out."

They hurried to the dining room, and they found Rhys, lying on the floor. His throat was cut open and he was dead. In the fireplace, the monkey was laughing and burning in the fire.

The guide ended his story, saying, "Even today, on cold, windy and stormy nights, all around the area, we can hear the screaming of Rhys and the laughter of the monkey as he burns in the fire. Some people have seen the monkey in the fireplace too. The man and the monkey are so evil, they cannot rest in peace."

It was a sunny day when I visited Carew Castle, but I felt very cold when I heard this story. I walked around the castle and went to the fireplace in the dining hall. It was very quiet. *Which ghost would I like to see?* I asked myself. *The beauty or the beast?*

The answer is very easy!

2. SHADOWS

Place: The Rhymney House Hotel, Tredegar, Blaenau Gwent

I left Pembrokeshire and travelled east to Blaenau Gwent. It took around an hour and a half to get there. It was a beautiful drive along roads surrounded by green fields and gentle hills. I had made a reservation at a hotel, not far from the Brecon Beacons National Park. Have you heard of this national park? It is very famous. It has mountains, hills, waterfalls, forests, lakes, and fields with Welsh mountain ponies. It is a very popular tourist place. Many people come here for hiking, cycling, windsurfing, fishing, rock-climbing and camping.

I arrived at the Rhymney House Hotel in the late afternoon. I checked in and went up to my room.

This is it. Number five, I thought. I went in, put my bags down and went down to the bar for a whisky. There was a group of three people - a woman and two men, sitting in the bar. They didn't sound local, their accents were English.

I sat at a nearby table with my whisky and newspaper. Then, I heard the woman say, "I hope we can see something tonight."

"I hope so too," said one of the men. "I think we will see shadows. Many people see shadows in the toilets, on the stairs, in the bar, and around the hotel. Some of the shadows are men, others are women and children."

The men and the woman looked around the room.

"I can't see anything," said the woman.

"No, it is too early," said the man.

I started to listen carefully.

The other man said, "I think room number five is the best room to see things, but unfortunately someone else is staying in there tonight."

I looked at them. *Room number five? That's my room!* I thought.

"Excuse me," I said. "I'm staying in room number five. Is there a problem with the room?"

The men and the woman looked at each other.

"Er, well…not really, but…" said the woman.

"Is there a ghost?" I asked.

She smiled.

"No, there isn't a ghost," said one of the men. "There are many ghosts!"

"And they are in room number five?" I asked.

"Well, some people think the ghosts enter and leave the hotel through room five," said the man. "It is like a door. A door between this life and the next life."

"Lucky me!" I said. Everyone laughed.

"Are you tourists?" I asked.

"We are ghost hunters," said the man. "We came to see some ghosts."

"That sounds interesting," I said. "Could you tell me about the ghosts here?"

"Of course," said the woman. She moved over to make some space.

"Come and sit with us. We'll tell you all about them."

I picked up my whisky and went over to their table. This is the story they told me.

The house was built in 1801, and it was owned by the Crawshay family. The family was rich, and they had servants. The head of the family, Richard Crawshay, was married, but he was having an affair with one of the servant girls. She became pregnant. She died soon after. People say she killed herself. Since then, many strange things have happened in the hotel.

Many people have seen a man riding a horse. The horse runs fast. It runs to the hotel doors. Some drivers on the road have stopped very quickly because they don't want to hit the man on the horse! And then, the man and the horse disappear…Of course, there is no man on a horse. It is a ghost.

The ghost hunters told me many stories. The one I remember the most is a very sad story. A previous owner of the hotel had a young daughter. One day, she said to her mother and father, "I like that beautiful lady."

"Which beautiful lady?" asked her mother.

"The beautiful lady who comes to my room every night."

Her mother and father said, "But there is no lady here! You are dreaming!"

"Yes, there is," said the girl. "And she is very kind. She always smiles and says goodnight to me."

Her mother and father laughed. They thought she was dreaming.

"No," said the girl. "I'm not dreaming. I see the woman every night."

One of the men said, "I think the woman is the ghost of the servant. Maybe she came to see the young girl every night because she was sad about her own child."

"That's sad," I said. "How about the man on the horse?"

"Maybe that is Richard, hurrying back to the house when he heard about the servant's death," said the other man.

It was getting late. I looked at my watch. "It's time for me to go to bed," I said.

"Good night Old Jack," said the woman. "We are going to stay awake, and watch for ghosts outside and on the stairs. Let us know if you see any ghosts in your room!"

I laughed. "I don't need to tell you," I said. "You will hear me. I will scream!"

Everyone laughed.

I went up the stairs. I looked at the wall. There was only one shadow. That was mine. I went into my room. I switched the lights on and sat on my bed. I looked around the room.

No, there are no ghosts in here, I thought.

I got undressed and got into bed. I switched the light off.

Maybe if I stay awake, I'll see something, I thought.

But I soon fell asleep. I didn't wake up until morning.

The next morning, I got up. I found my new friends sitting, eating breakfast. They looked very tired.

"Did you sleep well?" asked the woman.

"Yes, I did, thank you," I said. "Did you see anything?"

One of the men showed me his camera. "Look at this! What do you think this is?"

I looked at the picture. It was very dark, but I could see the white shadow of a young woman.

"It looks like a ghost!" I said. "Where did you see it?"

The man looked at me and smiled. "It was coming out of your room..."

3. THE ROPE

Place: The Skirrid Mountain Inn, Abergavenny, Monmouthshire

For our next story, we travel just 30 minutes along the road next to Brecon Beacons National Park and into Monmouthshire. We are going to the oldest pub in Wales. The pub is called The Skirrid Mountain Inn.

I have heard many stories about this pub. It is very famous around the world. It is famous because it is so old. It is 900 years old. It is also famous for its terrible and tragic history. And of course, its ghosts...

On the day of my visit, I arrived at the pub and parked my car. From the entrance, I could see the large mountain called Skirrid Mountain, or Ysgyryd Fawr in Welsh. Many people say this is a special mountain. They say that when Jesus Christ died, lightning hit the mountain and split the mountain into two pieces.

The word 'Skirrid' is Welsh. It means 'to shiver'. People say that the mountain shivered when it was hit by the lightning. I looked at the mountain and then at the pub. I shivered a little when I thought about the dark history of the pub.

I went inside. It was nearly lunch time, so I ordered some food and a cup of tea. I sat down near a young man. I took my guidebook out of my bag and started to look at it.

The young man looked over at me.

"Are you a tourist?" he asked.

"Yes, I am. I'm interested in this pub," I said.

"The oldest in Wales!" he said proudly.

"Yes, I know," I said. "I heard that it has a dark history."

"Oh yes," he said. "It was built nine hundred years ago. This room was the pub area, but upstairs, there was a courtroom. People who had committed crimes were taken to the court."

"What kind of crimes?" I asked.

"Many people used to steal sheep," said the man.

"And what happened to the people who stole sheep? Did they go to jail?" I asked.

The man laughed. "No, they didn't."

He looked at the barman. Then, he said to me, "Wait here a minute." He walked to the bar and spoke to the barman. Then, he came back.

"Come on!" he said. "The barman will bring your lunch when you come back. I want to show you something."

We walked out of the bar and he took me to the old wooden stairs. We went up the stairs.

"Look up," he said.

I looked up and saw a large piece of wood, with a rope attached to it. The rope was tied in a circle.

"The criminals didn't go to jail. They were hanged from the rope," said the man.

"They were hanged?" I asked. "For stealing sheep?"

"Yes. Some stole sheep, other people stole other things, or did other bad things. They were brought here, the rope was tied around their necks, and then they were pushed over the stairs. They died, while downstairs, people were drinking in the bar and having a good time."

I looked at the rope. "Is that the same rope?" I asked.

"No, it isn't," he said. "But look at the wood. It is damaged. People think it is the same wood. The rope damaged the wood when the criminals were hanged."

"How many criminals were hanged?" I asked.

"Around one hundred and eighty," he said.

I looked at the rope and the wood, and I listened to the people in the bar. They were talking and laughing and having a good time.

"It must have been terrible!" I said. "To die like that, when everyone was having a good time down in the bar!"

"I think so too," said the man. "Come on, let's get your lunch."

We went back into the bar and sat down.

"I read in my guidebook that there are many ghosts," I said, as I ate my lamb and potatoes.

"Oh yes, there are. The last hanging was in sixteen fifty eight. Since then, the spirits of the men have been returning. Some people have seen the ghost of a man called Crowther. He was hanged for sheep stealing. Some people have seen him on the stairs.

"And there are other ghosts. The hangman is here. He is not a nice ghost. He is very evil. And the courtroom judge is here too.

"Some visitors cannot breathe very well on the stairs. One woman walked up the stairs and suddenly, her neck became red! There were rope marks around her neck!"

"I don't believe it!" I said.

"It's true!" said the man.

He was enjoying telling me the stories.

"There are many more stories. Sometimes glasses in the kitchen fly across the room! People have seen money flying around the bar! And look over there!"

He pointed to the fireplace. There was a cup on it.

"What's that?" I asked.

"It's the Devil's cup," said the man.

"The Devil! Don't tell me the Devil is here too!" I said.

"I don't know, but the cup has a long history. The owner leaves some beer in the cup every night before he goes to bed. It is a tradition here. All the owners for hundreds of years have been doing it. Some mornings, the beer is gone!"

I think I need a beer, I thought. *But I can't have one. I have a long way to drive today.*

I finished my lunch, said 'thank you' to the man, and got in my car. As I drove north through the beautiful green land of Wales, I thought about the beer in the cup. Who drinks it? Maybe it is the ghost of the judge, happy to finish work in the courtroom. Or maybe it is the ghost of the hangman, having a beer after killing a man. Or maybe it is one of the criminals, having a final beer before death…

I shivered at that thought. Just like Skirrid Mountain, I shivered.

4. BONES AND BURIED SECRETS

Place: Gwydir Castle, Llanrwst, Conwy

I left South Wales and travelled north, to a small village near Snowdonia National Park. Wales' highest mountain, Mt Snowdon, is in this park. It is 1,085 metres high. Many people climb this mountain to enjoy the wonderful views. Some people say the views are the best in Britain. It has beautiful lakes and walking paths. But if you don't want to walk, you can take the mountain train to the top!

I had no time to go to the mountain on my trip. I planned to visit one of Wales' many castles. The castles of North Wales are very old. Many were built in the 12th and 13th centuries. Now, they are popular tourist spots. I visited Gwydir Castle, near the small market town of Llanrwst. It is different from the other castles. It looks like a large house. It was built around the 16th century. It was the home of the cousin of Queen Elizabeth I (the first). King Charles I and King George V (the fifth) stayed here. Now it is a family home. I wanted to see the castle and the famous gardens. The gardens are over 500 years old. One tree is 1000 years old!

Of course, I am not only interested in the gardens. I am interested in the secrets of Gwydir Castle. It has many secrets, and of course, ghosts. But not all the ghosts are human...

But first, let's start with the human ghosts. First, the ghost of a young woman who was murdered.

In the 17th century, the castle was owned by a man called Sir John Wynn. It seems that he was not a nice man. He did many bad things in his life. His worst crime was murder. He killed a servant girl at the

13

house. Why did he kill her? People say he was having an affair with the girl, and she became pregnant. Of course, Wynn was very angry. So, he killed her, and put her dead body inside a wall. Soon after, there was a bad smell in that area of the castle. People think Wynn moved the girl's body after that, because when people looked in the wall a long time later, they didn't find anything. Since then, many people have seen the ghost of a young woman. The ghost of the woman always brings a terrible smell…The smell of a dead body…

But what happened to the spirit of Wynn? Well, people have seen him too. His ghost walks around the castle. Why does he come back? What is he looking for? No one knows.

The dead girl's body was not found, but in the cellar, around twenty years ago, some bones were discovered. They were the bones of a large dog. A large dog had died, and it had been buried in the cellar. Maybe this is not so strange, but after the bones were found, something strange started to happen. People started to see a very large dog in the house and gardens. Some people still see it today.

I parked my car and walked to the entrance of the castle. It looked peaceful in the late afternoon sun. It was a beautiful old house.

But will the ghosts ever find peace? I thought. *Will the dead servant girl find peace? And what about the dog? Since its bones were moved, it hasn't been able to rest.*

I walked into the castle, thinking about bones and buried secrets.

5. ONE TRAGIC NIGHT

Place: Plas Mawr, Conwy

I travelled north, up to the beautiful Irish Sea coast. The north coast of Wales is a very popular tourist place. It has many seaside resorts and beautiful beaches. It is also home to one of the world's most wonderful 13th century towns - Conwy.

Conwy is most famous for its castle. For many years, English kings and Welsh princes fought over the area of Conwy. In the 13th century, King Edward I took control of the area, and built a castle. He didn't only build a castle, but he also built a town with walls around it. The walls were built as a defence.

Now, it is a popular sightseeing town. Of course, many people visit the castle, and enjoy the wonderful views of the sea. The town also has some interesting buildings. One popular place is the smallest house in Britain. It is only 3 metres high and 1.8 metres wide!

After looking around the castle, I went to a town house, called Plas Mawr. This house is in the middle of the town. 'Plas Mawr' means 'Great Hall' in English. It was built in the 16th century by a man called Robert Wynn. Do you remember John Wynn from Gwydir Castle? Well, Robert was his son. He was very rich, and he liked having parties. He had many parties here.

The house is wonderful. The outside walls are white, and there are towers. It is a town house, but, to me, it looks like a small castle.

As I walked around the rooms, I began to think of a story I heard a long time ago about Plas Mawr.

Let's go back to 1598. It was a cold and stormy night. Robert's wife, Dorothy, and his son were waiting for him to return.

"Let's go up to the tower. We can watch for him," said Dorothy. She took a candle, and she and her son went up to the tower. The tower was high, so they had to climb up a very steep ladder to get to the top. They sat next to the window, and looked out at the dark street.

"It's very windy and rainy. I hope he can come home safely," said Dorothy. She was very worried. She waited to hear Robert's horse and carriage coming down the road.

"I'm cold," said her son.

"Yes, it is cold," she said. "Shall we go downstairs and wait for him next to the fire?"

"Yes, let's," said her son.

They walked to the ladder. Dorothy picked up her young son and started to go down the ladder.

"Aahh!" she screamed as she fell down the ladder steps.

The maid, who was in the kitchen, heard the scream.

What was that? she thought. *It was Lady Dorothy! What's happened?*

She ran to the tower and found Dorothy and her son. They were badly hurt.

She sent another servant to the doctor's house.

"Tell the doctor to come quickly!" she said.

The main doctor was busy that night, so a young doctor came. They moved Dorothy and her son to a room called the Lantern Room. The young doctor looked at them.

He thought, *I cannot help them! They are too badly hurt. The lord will be very angry with me!*

He was a very young man, and he didn't have much experience. He panicked and tried to run away.

"Where are you going? You are not going anywhere! Help the lady and her son! Save them!" shouted the maid. She pushed the doctor into the room, closed the door, and locked it, so he could not escape.

When Robert returned that night, he ran up to the Lantern Room. He unlocked the door and found his wife and son. They were dead.

"Where is the doctor?" he shouted. "Where is he? I'll kill him!"

He looked around the room. The doctor was not there. The windows in that room were very small. So the doctor did not escape through the window. People say he tried to escape up the chimney. But after that, no one ever saw the doctor again. Some people say he died in the chimney. But no one found his body. It was a mystery.

Robert was very sad. He stayed in the room with his dead wife and son that night. The next morning, the maid was very worried. She went to the room and found Robert. He was dead. He had killed himself.

Since then, many strange things have happened in the house. People see the ghost of Robert. He is walking around the house. He looks very angry. People say he is looking for the doctor.

The doctor's ghost is here too. People hear strange noises from the chimney. It is like a man screaming. They say it is the ghost of the doctor, trying to escape.

As I walked out of the house into the warm afternoon sun, I looked up and thought about the ghosts.

I believe the ghost of Robert will stay in Plas Mawr until he finds the doctor. And the ghost of the doctor will stay until he can escape. Of course, the doctor will never escape, and Robert will never find him. The sad and tragic story of Plas Mawr will never end.

6. THE LADY BY THE SEA

Place: Prestatyn Sea, Prestatyn, Denbighshire

My trip to Wales was nearly finished. I left Conwy, and drove back towards England along the coast. It was a beautiful summer evening. Tourists were starting to go back to their hotels or homes after a long and happy day at the beach. I decided to stop at Prestatyn to see the sea. When I was a young boy, I often came to Prestatyn with my family for our summer holidays. I have many fine memories of Prestatyn and its wonderful sandy beaches.

I parked my car and walked along the sea coast. The Irish Sea was as blue as the sky, and the sea breeze was very pleasant. The sun was starting to set. As I was walking, I remembered a story I had heard when I was a child. The owner of a hotel told me this story about fifty years ago.

It was the story of the woman in the white dress. A long time ago, a family was walking along the sea coast. It was at the end of summer, and the sun was starting to set.

The boy looked at the empty beach and said, "Mother! Father! Look at that woman!"

His mother and father turned to look at the beach. They saw a woman, dressed in a long white dress. It was an old-fashioned dress, the style from about 100 years before.

The woman was walking slowly along the beach. The family stopped to look at her. The woman turned to look at them, and then she disappeared!

"She's gone! Where has she gone?" said the boy. His mother and

18

father could not answer. The woman had gone.

When the hotel owner told me this story, I didn't believe in ghosts. I said, "Maybe the family had been sitting in the sun for too long. Maybe they were tired and the sun was bright. I don't think it was a ghost."

The hotel owner looked at me and smiled. "Yes, Young Jack. Maybe you are right."

I forgot about that story, until around ten years ago, when I read a story about the lady in the newspaper. A man and his dog were walking along the sea coast one summer evening. Suddenly, a woman in a long white dress appeared in front of them. The man was very surprised and his dog was very frightened. He picked his dog up and started to walk very quickly. The woman turned around and started to follow him. He started to walk more quickly. He turned around to look at her, and he saw that the woman had no face…

After that, many people said they had seen the woman. It was always on summer evenings, just before sunset. Who is she? Why does she walk along the beach and the coast road in late summer at sunset? No one knows.

It was still warm, but I suddenly felt cold. I looked at my watch. It was getting late. *Time to go,* I thought. I turned around and walked back to my car. As I walked, I looked out at the beach and the sea.

What's that? I thought. There was a bright white light in the middle of the sea. I couldn't see very well, but it looked like a person. Then, it disappeared. Then, I saw another light. And another. I looked up at the sky, and I smiled.

Come on Old Jack! It's only the sun! You've been reading too many ghost stories! I thought.

I got in my car and left Wales as the sun set.

THANK YOU

Thank you for reading Old Jack's Ghost Stories from Wales. (Word count: 5,572) Old Jack hopes you enjoyed reading his stories.

For more information about the places in this book, please visit http://www.italk-youtalk.com. There is a page with maps and photographs of the places that Old Jack has written about.

If you would like to read more graded readers, please visit our website http://www.italkyoutalk.com

Other graded readers by Old Jack:
Old Jack's Ghost Stories from England (1)
Old Jack's Ghost Stories from England (2)
Old Jack's Ghost Stories from Scotland
Old Jack's Ghost Stories from Ireland
Old Jack's Ghost Stories from Japan

NOTES AND REFERENCES

1. The Beauty or the Beast?
Carew, Tenby, Pembrokeshire SA70 8SL
The story is based on information found on the following sites and in the following book:
http://www.pembrokeshirecoast.org.uk/?PID=353
(Retrieved July 2014)
http://en.wikipedia.org/wiki/Carew_Castle (Retrieved July 2014)
Redfern, Nick. The Most Mysterious Places on Earth (New York: The Rosen Publishing Group, 2014) pages 32-33

2. Shadows
The Rhymney House Hotel, Tredegar, Blaenau Gwent NP22 5QG
The story is based on information found on the following site:
http://www.glamorganparanormal.co.uk/the-rhymney-house-hotel.htm
(Retrieved August 2014)

3. The Rope
The Skirrid Mountain Inn, Llanvihangel Crucorney, Abergavenny, Monmouthshire, NP7 8DH
The story is based on information found on the following sites:
http://www.skirridmountaininn.co.uk/ (Retrieved August 2014)
http://en.wikipedia.org/wiki/The_Skirrid_Mountain_Inn (Retrieved August 2014)
http://www.glamorganparanormal.co.uk/The-Skirrid-Mountain-

inn.htm (Retrieved August 2014)

4. Bones and Buried Secrets
Gwydir Castle, Llanrwst, Conwy. LL26 0PN
The story is based on information found on the following sites:
http://www.gwydircastle.co.uk/home.htm (Retrieved August 2014)
http://www.gwydircastle.co.uk/ghosts.htm (Retrieved August 2014)
http://en.wikipedia.org/wiki/Gwydir_Castle (Retrieved August 2014)
http://www.hauntedrooms.co.uk/gwydir-castle-hotel (Retrieved August 2014)

5. One Tragic Night
Plas Mawr, High St, Conwy LL32 8DE
The story is based on information found on the following sites and in the following book:
http://www.conwy.com/plasmawr.html (Retrieved August 2014)
http://en.wikipedia.org/wiki/Plas_Mawr (Retrieved August 2014)
http://news.bbc.co.uk/2/hi/uk_news/wales/8560508.stm (Retrieved August 2014)
Underwood, Peter Haunted Wales (Gloucestershire: Amberley Publishing, 2012)

6. The Lady by the Sea
Prestatyn, Denbighshire
The story is based on information found on the following site:
http://news.bbc.co.uk/local/northeastwales/hi/people_and_places/newsid_8162000/8162533.stm (Retrieved August 2014)

ABOUT THE AUTHOR

I Talk You Talk Press is a Japan-based publisher of language textbooks, graded readers and language learning/teaching resources.

Our team is made up of highly experienced language teachers and translators, who have all studied at least one additional language to an advanced level.

This experience enables us to design our materials from the perspective of both the teacher and the learner. We consult with both teachers and language learners when designing our textbooks and graded readers, and test our materials extensively in the classroom before publication.

We are a fast-growing press, and currently publish graded readers for learners of English. We publish new graded readers monthly.

www.ingramcontent.com/pod-product-compliance
Lightning Source LLC
Chambersburg PA
CBHW022352040426
42449CB00006B/840